SHARK
Attack!

S0-DOO-075

CHRISTINE GRIFFITH

SCHOLASTIC INC.

The publisher thanks the following for their kind permission to use their photographs in this book:

Photographs ©: cover: Tim Davis/Corbis Images; page 1: Masa Ushioda/Seapics.com; page 3: Chris & Monique Fallows/OceanwideImages.com; page 4, 5: Biosphoto/Superstock, Inc.; page 6: George Karbus Photography/Media Bakery; page 7: holbox/Shutterstock, Inc.; page 8, 9: Stephen Frink/Corbis Images; page 10: Doug Perrine/Superstock, Inc.; page 11: Doug Perrine/Seapics.com; page 12: Minden Pictures/Superstock, Inc.; page 13 inset: Gary Bell/OceanwideImages.com; page 13 background: Minden Pictures/Superstock, Inc.; page 14: Stephan Kühn/Wikimedia; page 15: Greg Amptman/Shutterstock, Inc.; page 16, 17 background: Louise Murray/Alamy Images; page 17 inset: Doug Perrine/Seapics.com; page 18, 19: Jim Abernethy/Getty Images; page 20, 21: Amanda Cotton/Alamy Images; page 22: Simon Hathaway/Alamy Images; page 23: Jezperklauzen/iStockphoto; page 24, 25: John Borthwick/Getty Images; page 26, 27: Angelo Cavalli/Alamy Images; page 28, 29 background: Mark Conlin/Getty Images; page 29 inset: Clay Coleman/Science Source; page 30, 31: Tim Clark/Newscom; page 32 top: arlindo71/iStockphoto; page 32 center top: f8grapher/Shutterstock, Inc.; page 32 center bottom: PeteMuller/iStockphoto; page 32 bottom: ShaneGross/iStockphoto

ISBN 978-0-545-72493-7

12 11 10 9 8 7 6 5 4 3 2 1   14 15 16 17 18 19/0
Printed in the U.S.A.   40
First edition, September 2014

Sharks look like scary monsters.
But how dangerous are they?
Get ready to learn
the real story about
shark attacks!

Sharks are one of the top hunters in the ocean.

Very few animals attack them!

But sharks are not monsters.

Sharks help keep the ocean clean and healthy. They eat weak and sick animals.

Sharks hunt fish, seals, sea lions, sea turtles, and other animals. But sharks don't normally hunt people.

Sharks will take a bite of something to see if it is food. People dump a lot of trash into the ocean. So, sharks have eaten some strange things.

Here are some things that people have found inside sharks:

- coats
- boots
- a drum
- wood
- cans
- dolls

Most sharks leave people alone. When sharks do bite people, it is often a mistake.

Shark bites usually don't kill
people. Sharks cause only
about ten deaths every year.
When you think of all the
people in the world, ten is
not many.

Most shark attacks happen to surfers. Look at these pictures and you can see why. From below, a person on a surfboard may look a lot like a sea lion. Sharks like to eat sea lions.

To a shark, this surfer may look like a sea lion.

Splashing water also attracts sharks. To a shark, splashing means that an animal is hurt or sick. That would be an easy meal for a shark.

Real sea lion

Sometimes, people cause sharks to bite. People catch sharks in their fishing nets along with other fish. Sharks end up in the fishing boat by mistake.

Some kinds of sharks swim near the sandy bottom. People can step on one by accident.

Some people get close to sharks on purpose. They feed a shark or grab its fin. That's dangerous. Sharks are wild animals.

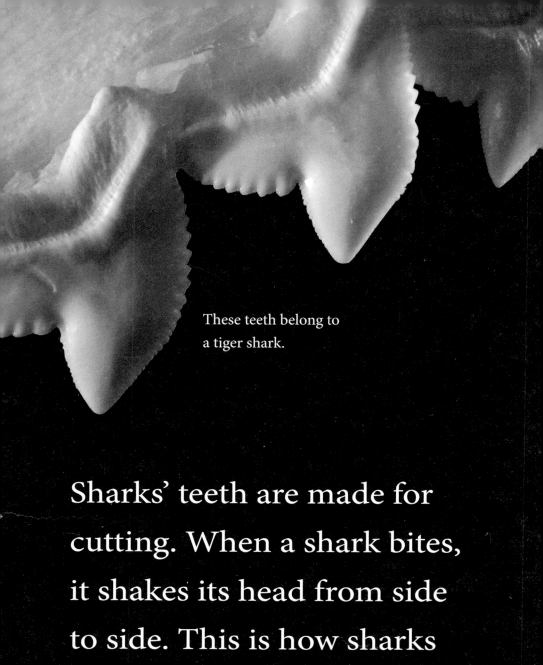

These teeth belong to
a tiger shark.

Sharks' teeth are made for
cutting. When a shark bites,
it shakes its head from side
to side. This is how sharks
tear their food.

The most dangerous sharks are great white sharks, bull sharks, and tiger sharks.

Great white sharks are big and powerful. Some people say they are the most dangerous sharks. They are about four times as long as you are. The largest great white sharks weigh about as much as a car.

Tiger sharks will eat almost anything. After they bite a person, they probably will not swim away. Some people think that tiger sharks are the most dangerous sharks.

What do you think?

Sharks sometimes hunt for food where people go to swim. People look for sharks from boats and airplanes. If sharks are nearby, signs tell people to stay out of the water.

In Western Australia, people have tagged more than three hundred sharks. These tags can send messages on the Internet. If a shark gets too close to shore, the tag sends a message to warn people.

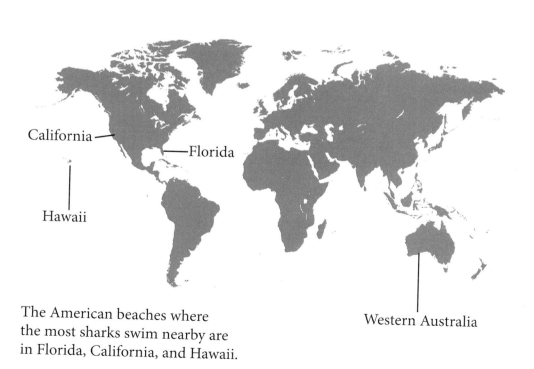

California —

—Florida

Hawaii

Western Australia

The American beaches where the most sharks swim nearby are in Florida, California, and Hawaii.

At age thirteen, Bethany
Hamilton was a star surfer from
Hawaii. Bethany was surfing one
day when a tiger shark attacked.
She was hurt, but she was lucky.
The attack was not deadly.
Bethany's friends and
family rushed to help her.

It took time for Bethany to get well. But today she is a star surfer again. Her story was made into a book and a movie.

Here are the best ways to avoid sharks. Stay out of the water in the morning and evening. That's when sharks like to eat. Never swim by yourself.

Don't wear shiny clothing or jewelry in the water. Sharks may think you are a fish.

If you have a cut, stay out of the water. Sharks can smell blood from far away.

If you see a shark, leave the water right away. Stay calm. Try not to splash around.

If a shark is about to bite, you can fight back. Hit the shark in the nose, eyes, or gills. Those are the places that will hurt the shark most.

Sharks use their gills to breathe underwater.

gills

People have new ways to stay safe from sharks. By using special clothing and surfboards, surfers don't look like shark food.

Do magnets keep sharks away? Some people think so. A magnet dropped in salt water makes a little bit of electricity. Does this bother sharks? Maybe!

Sharks are dangerous animals.
But they will never hurt
most people.
Look at this chart. Sharks are
at the bottom of the list!

ANIMAL	AVERAGE NUMBER OF DEADLY ATTACKS IN THE US IN A YEAR
Bees, Wasps, and Hornets	57
Dogs	28
Spiders	8
Sharks	1